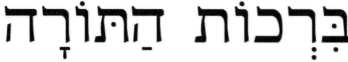

בִּרְכוֹת הַתּוֹרָה

Have you seen the Torah's elaborate cover and ornaments—its rich silver embroidery on fine fabric, tiny bells adorning brass or silver handle ornaments, and fancy breastplate? When the Torah reaches the reader's table after it has been carried through the congregation, the rabbi or Torah reader removes the covering and ornaments, sets the Torah on the table, and unrolls it to that week's פָּרָשָׁה—Torah portion.

Each *parashah* is divided into sections, or readings. For each section, one or more congregants are called up to the Torah to say two blessings—one before the Torah reader begins to read that section, and one after the reader has finished. The honor of being called up to recite these blessings is called an עֲלִיָּה ("going up"). The blessing before the Torah reading has two parts. The first part is the Bar'chu, a call to the congregation to praise God. The second part thanks God for choosing us to receive the gift of the Torah.

BLESSING BEFORE THE TORAH READING

Practice reading the blessing aloud.

1. בָּרְכוּ אֶת־יְיָ הַמְבֹרָךְ.
2. בָּרוּךְ יְיָ הַמְבֹרָךְ לְעוֹלָם וָעֶד.
3. בָּרוּךְ אַתָּה, יְיָ אֱלֹהֵינוּ, מֶלֶךְ הָעוֹלָם,
4. אֲשֶׁר בָּחַר־בָּנוּ מִכָּל־הָעַמִּים,
5. וְנָתַן־לָנוּ אֶת־תּוֹרָתוֹ.
6. בָּרוּךְ אַתָּה, יְיָ, נוֹתֵן הַתּוֹרָה.

Praise Adonai, who is praised.
Praised is Adonai, who is praised forever and ever.
Praised are You, Adonai our God, Ruler of the world,
for choosing us from all the nations
and giving us God's Torah.
Praised are You, Adonai, who gives us the Torah.

בָּחַר

chose (choosing)

בָּנוּ

us

מִכָּל

from all

הָעַמִּים

the nations

וְנָתַן

and gave (and giving)

לָנוּ

to us

תּוֹרָתוּ

God's Torah

נוֹתֵן

gives

MATCH GAME

Connect each Hebrew word to its English meaning.

us	בָּחַר
and gave (and giving)	בָּנוּ
chose (choosing)	מִכָּל הָעַמִּים
to us	וְנָתַן
God's Torah	נוֹתֵן
gives	לָנוּ
from all the nations	תּוֹרָתוּ

This Torah mantle is adorned with a quote from Leviticus 25:10, which also appears on the Liberty Bell in Philadelphia.

It is no easy task to read from the Torah. You must be trained to read Hebrew fluently, and without vowels or punctuation, in order to read without mistakes. What's more, in many synagogues the Torah portion is chanted using special musical inflections or melodies called trope. The Torah reader (בַּעַל קְרִיאָה, for a man or a boy; בַּעֲלַת קְרִיאָה, for a woman or a girl) often prepares for the reading by practicing in a *tikkun*, a book in which the words of the Torah appear twice—in one column they appear in regular Hebrew print with vowels and punctuation, and in the second column, the text looks just like the Torah itself.

Sometimes, the Torah reader is the Bar Mitzvah or Bat Mitzvah, whose family members are given the honor of an *aliyah*—reciting the blessings before and after the sections in the Torah reading. If you read Torah when you celebrate becoming Bar or Bat Mitzvah, *you* may learn how to read trope.

Here is the way Hebrew letters look in a Torah scroll.

אבגדהוזחטיכךלמסנןסעפףצץקרשת

Connect each Torah letter below to the matching printed letter.

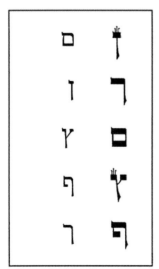

Prayer Building Blocks

Read the first two lines of the Torah blessing. Do you recognize them?

בָּרְכוּ אֶת־יְיָ הַמְבֹרָךְ.

בָּרוּךְ יְיָ הַמְבֹרָךְ לְעוֹלָם וָעֶד.

The Torah reading begins with the בָּרְכוּ—the Call to Worship, the official opening of the prayer service. Why do you think the blessing before the Torah reading begins with the בָּרְכוּ?

_____

_____

Words built on the root ברכ have "praise" or "bless" as part of their meaning. Circle all the words in the בָּרְכוּ that are built on the root ברכ.

This root means _____ or _____.

Now read the next part of the Torah blessing.

בָּרוּךְ אַתָּה, יְיָ אֱלֹהֵינוּ, מֶלֶךְ הָעוֹלָם,

אֲשֶׁר בָּחַר־בָּנוּ מִכָּל־הָעַמִּים, וְנָתַן־לָנוּ אֶת־תּוֹרָתוֹ.

Underline the six words that are found at the beginning of most בְּרָכוֹת.

אֲשֶׁר בָּחַר בָּנוּ "who chose us" ("for choosing us")

אֲשֶׁר means "who."

בָּחַר means "chose."

בָּנוּ means "us."

Who chose us to receive the Torah? _____

To whom does "us" refer? _____

4

וְנָתַן לָנוּ אֶת תּוֹרָתוֹ

"and gave us God's Torah" ("and giving us God's Torah")

וְנָתַן means "and gave."

וְ is a prefix meaning _____.

נָתַן means _____ .

לָנוּ means "to us."

תּוֹרָתוֹ is made up of two word-parts: תּוֹרָה and the word ending וֹ ("his").

Because God is neither male nor female, we translate תּוֹרָתוֹ as "God's Torah."

What did God give us? _____

Write your answer in Hebrew. _____

CROSSWORD

Read the Hebrew clues and fill in the correct English words.

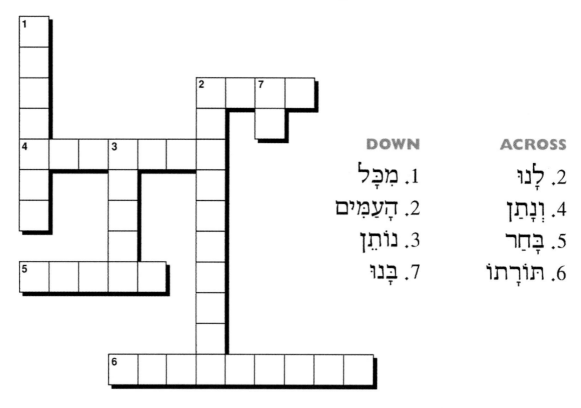

DOWN

1. מִכָּל

2. הָעַמִּים

3. נוֹתֵן

7. בָּנוּ

ACROSS

2. לָנוּ

4. וְנָתַן

5. בָּחַר

6. תּוֹרָתוֹ

FACTS AND FIGURES ABOUT THE TORAH READING

- The Torah (also called the Five Books of Moses) is divided into 54 portions (פָּרָשׁוֹת).

- It takes exactly one year to read the whole Torah. We begin reading the first book, Genesis (בְּרֵאשִׁית), on Simḥat Torah, and complete reading the last book, Deuteronomy (דְּבָרִים), one year later on the following Simḥat Torah. We then begin all over again.

- The last person called to the Torah on Shabbat is known as the *maftir* (for a man or a boy) or the *maftirah* (for a woman or a girl). This is often the Bar Mitzvah or Bat Mitzvah. The *maftir* or *maftirah* recites the blessings before and after the reading of the last few verses of the Torah portion, and then chants a portion from Prophets called the *haftarah*.

Answer the following questions:

1. How many portions (פָּרָשׁוֹת) are contained in the Torah? _____

2. On which holiday do we finish reading the Torah and begin all over again?

   _____

3. Explain what the *maftir* or *maftirah* does.

   _____

   _____

4. How do you think it feels to be the *maftir* or *maftirah*? Why?

   _____

   _____

BLESSING AFTER THE TORAH READING

The blessing we say after the Torah reader has finished reading that section of the Torah praises God for giving us the Torah of truth and eternal life. Although our bodies cannot live forever, by reading the Torah and passing it and its lessons down to our children and then to their children, we keep Torah and we keep our heritage alive forever. The chain of tradition that began when Moses and the Israelites received the Torah almost 3,500 years ago lives on as we hear its words each week.

Practice reading the blessing said after the Torah reading.

1. בָּרוּךְ אַתָּה, יְיָ אֱלֹהֵינוּ, מֶלֶךְ הָעוֹלָם,

2. אֲשֶׁר נָתַן־לָנוּ תּוֹרַת אֱמֶת

3. וְחַיֵּי עוֹלָם נָטַע בְּתוֹכֵנוּ.

4. בָּרוּךְ אַתָּה, יְיָ, נוֹתֵן הַתּוֹרָה.

Praised are You, Adonai our God, Ruler of the world,
who gave us the Torah of truth,
and implanted within us eternal life.
Praised are You, Adonai, who gives us the Torah.

תּוֹרַת

Torah of

אֱמֶת

truth

וְחַיֵּי

and life (of)

עוֹלָם

eternal, world

PHRASE MATCH

Connect each Hebrew phrase to its English meaning.

and eternal life	לְעוֹלָם וָעֶד
ruler of the world	תּוֹרַת אֱמֶת
forever and ever	וְחַיֵּי עוֹלָם
Torah of truth	מֶלֶךְ הָעוֹלָם

When we help someone in need, or perform any other mitzvah, we are keeping the words of the Torah alive.

WHAT'S MISSING?

Fill in the missing Hebrew words in the prayer.

בָּרוּךְ אַתָּה, יְיָ אֱלֹהֵינוּ, מֶלֶךְ הָעוֹלָם,

אֲשֶׁר נָתַן־לָנוּ _____ _____
Torah of truth

_____ _____ נָטַע בְּתוֹכֵנוּ.
and eternal life

בָּרוּךְ אַתָּה, יְיָ, _____ הַתּוֹרָה.
gives

Prayer Building Blocks

אֲשֶׁר נָתַן לָנוּ תּוֹרַת אֱמֶת

"who gave us the Torah of truth"

נָתַן לָנוּ means _____.

תּוֹרַת אֱמֶת means "Torah of truth."

תּוֹרַת is a combination word that means "Torah of."

אֱמֶת means "truth."

Complete the Hebrew phrase: _____ אֲשֶׁר נָתַן לָנוּ

What did God give us? _____

Why do you think we refer to the Torah as "Torah of truth"?

_____

_____

וְחַיֵּי עוֹלָם "and eternal life"

וְחַיֵּי means "and a life of."

וְ is a prefix meaning _____.

חַיֵּי means "a life of."

The word for "life" is חַיִּים. (Do you know the toast "לְחַיִּים!"—"To Life!"?)

עוֹלָם means "eternal."

עוֹלָם also means "world."

וְחַיֵּי עוֹלָם means _____.

Read the following sentences and underline עוֹלָם in each one.

1. וְשִׁבְחֲךָ אֱלֹהֵינוּ מִפִּינוּ לֹא יָמוּשׁ לְעוֹלָם וָעֶד.

2. אֲדוֹן עוֹלָם אֲשֶׁר מָלַךְ בְּטֶרֶם כָּל יְצִיר נִבְרָא.

3. יִתְבָּרַךְ שִׁמְךָ בְּפִי כָל חַי תָּמִיד לְעוֹלָם וָעֶד.

4. וַאֲנַחְנוּ נְבָרֵךְ יָהּ מֵעַתָּה וְעַד עוֹלָם.

5. נְקַדֵּשׁ אֶת שִׁמְךָ בָּעוֹלָם, כְּשֵׁם שֶׁמַּקְדִּישִׁים אוֹתוֹ בִּשְׁמֵי מָרוֹם.

6. אֵל חַי וְקַיָּם תָּמִיד יִמְלֹךְ עָלֵינוּ לְעוֹלָם וָעֶד.

CHALLENGE QUESTION

Reread the blessing on page 7.

Describe the theme—or main idea—of this blessing, which is recited after the Torah reading.

_____

_____

_____

ALIYAH

Why do we use the term עֲלִיָּה ("going up")? We *go up* to the *bimah* when we are called to recite the blessings before and after each section of the Torah reading. We also *go up* in the eyes of the congregation when we receive this honor. And we *go up*, or move closer, to God.

You may have heard the word עֲלִיָּה in a different context. Going to live in Israel is called עֲלִיָּה (we "make *aliyah*"). We don't just *move* to the Holy Land, we *go up* to it.

The number of עֲלִיּוֹת in each Torah portion depends on the day it is read. For example, on Mondays and Thursdays there are three עֲלִיּוֹת, on Yom Kippur there are six, and on Shabbat morning there are usually seven. The number of עֲלִיּוֹת indicates the level of holiness of the day. In this case, Shabbat is even holier than Yom Kippur!

In some congregations, each person honored with an *aliyah* receives a special blessing of well-being, called a מִי שֶׁבֵּרַךְ. In this blessing, we ask God to protect the person from illness and distress, and to bless him or her with good health and success. Another version of the prayer, said during the Torah service, asks for the well-being of sick congregants, their loved ones, and friends.

New immigrants making *aliyah* to the State of Israel

FLUENT READING

Each line below contains a word you know. Practice reading the lines.

.1 בָּרוּךְ שֶׁנָּתַן תּוֹרָה לְעַמּוֹ יִשְׂרָאֵל בִּקְדֻשָּׁתוֹ.

.2 יְהִי שֵׁם יְיָ מְבֹרָךְ, מֵעַתָּה וְעַד עוֹלָם.

.3 הוּא נוֹתֵן לֶחֶם לְכָל בָּשָׂר.

.4 תּוֹרָה וּמִצְוֹת, חֻקִּים וּמִשְׁפָּטִים אוֹתָנוּ לִמַּדְתָּ.

.5 שֶׁכָּל דְּבָרָיו אֱמֶת וָצֶדֶק.

.6 וְתִתֶּן לָנוּ חַיִּים אֲרֻכִּים, חַיִּים שֶׁל שָׁלוֹם,
     חַיִּים שֶׁל טוֹבָה, חַיִּים שֶׁל בְּרָכָה.

.7 כַּכָּתוּב בְּתוֹרָתֶךְ: יְיָ יִמְלֹךְ לְעֹלָם וָעֶד.

.8 אֵין לָנוּ מֶלֶךְ אֶלָּא אָתָּה.

.9 חַיִּים שֶׁתְּהֵי בָנוּ אַהֲבַת תּוֹרָה וְיִרְאַת שָׁמַיִם.

.10 כִּי אַתָּה שׁוֹמֵעַ תְּפִלַּת עַמְּךָ יִשְׂרָאֵל.

ISBN 978-0-87441-765-4

Photographs: Torah Mantle by Peachy Levy, HUCSM (2), Gila Gevirtz (8), Israel Ministry of Tourism (11). ISBN 978-0-87441-765-4 (Birchot HaTorah); Manufactured in the United States of America

T0265441

9 780874 417654 >